Every Small Breeze

Every Small Breeze

Poems by

Marjorie Moorhead

© 2023 Marjorie Moorhead. All rights reserved.
This material may not be reproduced in any form, published,
reprinted, recorded, performed, broadcast,
rewritten or redistributed without
the explicit permission of Marjorie Moorhead.
All such actions are strictly prohibited by law.

Cover art detail of a painting by Max-Henry Moorhead,
photographed by Marjorie Moorhead
Cover design by Shay Culligan

ISBN: 978-1-63980-449-8
Library of Congress Control Number: 2023946055

Kelsay Books
502 South 1040 East, A-119
American Fork, Utah 84003
Kelsaybooks.com

For
Rob, Max-Henry, John;
Martha, Charles, Barbara, Nancy

Also by Marjorie Moorhead

Survival: Trees, Tides, Song
Survival Part 2: Trees, Birds, Ocean, Bees

Acknowledgments

Grateful acknowledgement goes to the editors of the following journals in which poems in this book first appeared, sometimes in earlier versions or with different titles:

Amethyst Review: "When Blue Breaks," "Head in the Clouds"
Bloodroot Literary Magazine: "Every Small Breeze"
Consilience Journal: "Arctic Breezes in May"
COVID-19 Archive: Images and Stories From Vermont: "As the Spring Birds Sing"
HIV Here & Now: "April Locket," "Ars Poetica," "Before and After," "COMPROMISE/D," "Counting," "From AIDS to Covid," "Like a Ballet Star," "Long Term Survival," "Nuyorican in Vermont," "Re-Traumatized," "Remembering Jorge," "Set You Free," "Since the Epidemic," "Coronavirus Diary V," "What Are Some Other Side Effects of This Drug?"
Journal Of Expressive Writing: "Turn the Corner"
Kissing Dynamite: "Wash and Overlay"
Lifelines: "All Storms"
Literary North: "That Which Makes Us Joyful"
Moist Poetry Journal: "In a Riparian Zone," "Sweet Things"
Poems in the Afterglow: "Another Chickadee Poem," "11/7/2020"
Porter House Review: "Caught by Chance"
The Rising Phoenix Review: "December Clear"
Tiny Seed Literary Journal: "Red," "A Large Bear Swims," "We Hunt for Mercy"
Verse-Virtual: "A Poet I Know," "Coronavirus Diary II," "Descending on Us All," "Insomnia Song," "Seed Sower," "Solace, "Wild Goats of Llandudno," "Winter of My Sixtieth Year"
What Rough Beast: "Because an Invitation," "Before It Goes, Remember," "Borders," "Colored Birds Bouquet," "Connection," "Coronavirus Diary," "Coronavirus Diary III," "Coronavirus Diary IV," "Glass Half-Full Today," "Only Love Songs," "Ovine," "Portal," "Practice," "Rat-a-Tat Rain," "Shout

the summer of 2020," "Starlight in My Pocket," "Walking with the Wind," "What Is Freedom?," "When the Pandemic Is Over"
Writing in a Woman's Voice: "Gently Let This Day"

These poems appeared in the following anthologies and chapbooks:

Birchsong: Poetry Centered in Vermont, Volume II: "All of a Sudden" "East Thetford, VT"
Covid Spring: Granite State Pandemic Poems: "Woman Under Covid-19"
From the Ashes: An International Anthology of Womxn's Poetry: "Wild Bindweed, Yarrow, and Me"
Protest 2021: "M.O. the Poet"
Survival Part 2: Trees, Birds, Ocean, Bees (chapbook): "Wishing Well"

I'd like to extend my gratitude and appreciation to Indolent Books' Michael Broder for early encouragement. Thank you also to poet James Diaz for his editorial input and kindness.

Heartfelt thank you to James Crews, Diane Seuss, Risa Denenberg, and Pam Broadley for their thoughtful words about this book!

My gratitude and thanks go to each kind and open-minded editor who encouraged me by publishing my work, and to the many poets who have taught and inspired me by example, workshop, or both.

Thank you to the Fine Arts Work Center (FAWC) in Provincetown and to director of education programs Kelle Groom for a 2019 Poetry Week summer workshop scholarship.

Thank you Ellen Bass, Shyft at Mile High, James Crews & Danusha Laméris, Hudson Valley Writers Center, and FAWC for scholarships allowing people with financial need to attend craft talk/workshops on Zoom.

Thank you Dartmouth Creative Writing, Norwich Bookstore, Bookstock, Poetry & Pie, Canaan St. Meeting House Readings, Hartford, Thetford, Norwich, Howe libraries for bringing amazing poets to this area for readings and inviting the public to join.

Thank you Catherine O'Brian, for starting my journey with Opening Windows, a poetry class for 55-and-over, which I joined with my mother, and then for inviting me, years later, to guest teach one of your classes.

Thank you Joni Cole for teaching the gift of unedited "free writing," and Pam B. for facilitating our WISE women prompt writers group for years.

Thank you to 4th Friday Poets, my local poet group who faithfully meet and support each other's work. It lifts my spirits every time.

Contents

Fields and Verges	17
Starlight in My Pocket	21
Portal	22
Me	23
East Thetford, VT	24
All of a Sudden	25
All Storms	26
Rat-a-Tat Rain	27
Borders	28
Because an Invitation	29
Set You Free	30
Counting	31
Walking with the Wind	32
Caught by Chance	33
Long Term Survival	34
Seed Sower	35
December Clear	36
April Locket	37
Remembering Jorge	38
Like a Ballet Star	39
A Poet I Know	40
Laura's Lights	41
Provincetown Night	42
Colored Birds Bouquet	43
What Is Freedom?	44
Ovine	45
Practice	46
Wild Bindweed, Yarrow, and Me	47
Glass Half-Full Today	48
Wash and Overlay	49
As the Spring Birds Sing	50
Coronavirus Diary	51
In the Silence	52
Before, and After	53

Coronavirus Diary II	54
Descending on Us All	55
Wild Goats of Llandudno *Lockdown*	56
Re-Traumatized	57
Woman Under Covid-19	58
Coronavirus Diary V	59
Coronavirus Diary III	60
Coronavirus Diary IV	61
Arctic Breezes in May	62
Shout	63
Only Love Songs	64
When the Pandemic Is Over	65
Connection	67
Before It Goes, Remember	68
Red	69
11/7/2020	70
From AIDS to Covid	71
Since the Epidemic	72
Nuyorican in Vermont	73
What Are Some Other Side Effects of This Drug?	75
Ars Poetica	76
COMPROMISE/D	77
M.O. the Poet	78
We Hunt for Mercy	79
Another Chickadee Poem	80
Winter of My Sixtieth Year	81
That Which Makes Us Joyful	82
Wishing Well	83
Turn the Corner	84
A Large Bear Swims	85
Insomnia Song	86
Gently Let This Day	87
Solace	88
Arise	89

Moon, Deer, Mountains, Stars	90
Every Small Breeze	91
Sweet Things	92
The heart is not	93
When blue breaks	94
In a Riparian Zone	96
Head in the Clouds	97

Fields and Verges

Soothing water feeds the weed flowers.
Possibly, they need it most. Out there on their own
in the verges; scattered in a field. Wild.
Bubble, bubble, bubble; rain sinks to soil.
Steep in it, thistle, vetch, and clover.
Goldenrod, yarrow, aster,
milkweed, sumac, rudbeckia,
wild carrot, periwinkle, phlox.
Now sing. Show your tones.
Shine, with spiky leaves or smooth,
petals wide or pointed.
Honor gifts from ancestor seeds.
Shout out your yellows, pinks, purples
and blues.

Wake up and ache for your life.
—Natalie Diaz, "Postcolonial Love Poem"

Starlight in My Pocket

A song I'm learning says, *Catch a falling star,*
says, *put it in your pocket.* A clue:
keep it there for when needed, when things look blue.

Keep it for when troubles start growing,
creating a fright.
The song says, *and they just might.*

Troubles are easy to forget without trying,
the lyrics say. All that's needed: *a pocketful of starlight.*
Who's got starlight?! Will it help when I'm crying?

I keep a rock from the beach in my pocket.
Smooth, to rub. Silky soft surface.
Dissipates worry. Works; don't knock it.

Smoothed by the sea, not a scratch or scar.
Is it my starlight? Gives comfort,
like music while driving in the car.

Trees whizz by. I sing out, at the top of my lungs
releasing anxiety, things that have stung.
Not kept in reserve "for a rainy day,"

this orb, too, in my pocket, helps worries fall away.
An everyday tool. With me while I cruise,
in car, or on foot, singing the blues.

Portal

There's a bruise in the crook
of my arm
a portal
the thinnest skin

access
to my heart
a bruise, where the needle went in
and prodded

trying to get blood to flow
a letting
necessary to check
and see how I am doing.

The bruise
a yin-yang now of purple and yellow
takes me back
The day I saw them on your arm,

grayish black   a whole row
tracks   the mark of a journey
a descent
a road to the end

an escape route
When you stepped on that path
there was no leaving it
you managed to stray   for awhile

you stayed
        But then,
you left
    for good.

Me

Warrior me knows days like this pass.
Days like this feel like a bruise.
Warrior me is wise from battle,
having faced death so close as to learn its odor.

Wise me knows vanity has been set aside,
like an old trunk abandoned on the sidewalk, shed forever.
Wise Old Trunk me knows light is inside, found in the breath—
in, then out, of each moment.

My turtle shell formed from incurable disease and each drug used
to fight it.
An outer leathery coating for one
whose tenderness is soft and squishy away from the air,
revealed only when tipped and pried at, below the surface.

Turtle me knows there are bruise days but there will be
days of connection, with music, poetry, laughter,
when Invisible Me and Creative Me
dance.

East Thetford, VT

Walking saved me years ago
Walking the same route every day
Day after day season after season.

Early morning; mid-day; dusk

It was only a mile or so
down to the farm and back
a flat road off the main road; probably once a train-rail.

Grasses; corn; clouds

Backdrop-sky for stone house, wood barn
tall stalks, big trees, lilacs.
At sunset simple silhouettes framing pink and orange-purple
    swaths.

Smells; wind; birds

My steps, my thoughts;
the rhythm of stride, breath.
Watching and noting details. What changes; what stays constant.

Dirt; puddles; tracks

Relationship with land can be just a road
claimed with each footstep.
You know it, because you walk it.

Repetition; observation; devotion.

All of a Sudden

Just like that, leaves are red in swaths
tinted by a perennial brush.
Autumn hues orange, gold, yellowed.
All of a sudden, it's cold in morning's hush
and dark. Fog hangs in valleys until the chill has mellowed.

Just like that, sun seems precious.
A limited commodity to be hoarded.
An aid in the battle against scarcity.
All of a sudden, geese fly overhead, squadron sorted,
sailing the clouds toward warmth, squawking commands with
    levity.

Just like that, I tug for my share of sheet
in morning's chill, instead of pushing it off
to avoid the humid sweat of August.
All of a sudden, t-shirts aren't enough;
long pants are pulled from drawers; thick sweaters become a must.

Just like that my little blond-haired boys look like men.
At the table, my husband and I shadowed with long silence.
Parents seem brittle like branches; dry, and primed to snap.
All of a sudden, life's like a movie; scenes gone by in sequence.
Family pets grown old. I rock them,
our small moments and big events piled in my lap.

All Storms

We met before the Internet!
Before it was carried in every pocket,
consulted for every question.

Dying of a disease that had no cure, denied
a roadmap for survival, I was convinced
this status precluded romantic love.

And then you appeared. So unlikely!
Medicine improved; death sentence amended.
We embraced. Came into balance,

filled in each other's halves. Wholeness
brought a child, and then his brother.
Such miraculous blessings, full of wonder!

How could it be we've grown old together?
Parented, shared families' sagas. Cultivated
talents and imperfection. Not clear

if we'll navigate every rocky road. Wind blows
from all direction. Keep hold my hand, and I'll clasp
yours . . . maybe we'll weather all storms.

Because you lifted me from barren desert,
and held me until I could grow,
because I let you do so,

do I request that you remain?
Touchstone. Pillar. Forever.
Is this fair to wonder?

Rat-a-Tat Rain

Sitting in a room where raindrops reverb.
Pinging hard, like machine gun fire today.
Disturb pitter-patter rapid-fire style.
Bump stock speed: no delay.

Picking off leaves one by one.
Red, golden, orange, brown.
Torn from branch and stem; each bullet drop
tears one down.

Shapes gather to form a blanket, wet.
Lay atop autumn grass and let
death's gleam shimmer and wink.

The joke: Winter must come. Don't think
it won't. All will slow and fester;
in small places sequester.

Huddle for warmth and shelter!
The Ice Queen cometh; we've all felt her.
"Shelter in Place"! "Rat-a-tat" there it is again!

In meditation; legs crossed, spine straight
that's when I hear it: harsh rain.
Usually too busy to let it into my brain,

in silence and full presence
I hear the drops above.
An introduction to this Season's essence:

Light to dark,
fluid to frozen, active to hibernating,
abundant to empty; stark.

Borders

For the second time in a short while
I find myself sitting under rain drops.
The sound sweeps in and away as a hard pattering
    like hooves of battalion horses moving through.
A windblown storm cloud.

Previously: a steady pounding coupled with thunder and lightning.
I did not feel threatened then; though later came reports hail had
    fallen!
There was a terror attack in London. My sister and brother-in-law
    are there.
I find myself thinking it's for the best my son is leaving Manhattan
    for Queens.

We could be under rain drops anywhere. Tragedy visits anywhere.
Where do we find ourselves? Borders in our minds.
What we could fathom and what we could not.
Rising sea levels. Depleting ice caps. Dividing lines.

Because an Invitation

Because I'm up before the dawn,
I see rosy clouds appear as sun breaks.
Because it is late November,

all is couched in a hazy cold moisture cluster;
festering, gathering, waiting for weight
to bring it down as snow.

Few leaves hanging on.
Most have hit the earth,
skittered and clattered dryly away.

Now tree skeletons stand tall and proud,
showing beautiful silhouettes
on a cold air screen.

Will they get a blanket?
How thick will it be?
A many snowflaked quilt, joined in unique pattern.

Because I worry about such things,
I think about the shoveling out,
and the shuttering in.

Because it seems like old school survival;
boots pulled over wool,
ear flaps, gloves, scarves,
tissues and hot soup at hand.

Will the frail and infirm survive?
To be warmed by spring,
and hear its song?
Because an invitation is on its way
for the hardy.

Set You Free

for Jorge Soto Sanchez

Clave! tap-tap-tap, tap-tap
tap-tap-tap, tap-tap!
In 1984, we listen happily.
You tell me of salsa's rhythm—Willie Colón, Celia Cruz
Rubén Blades y Seis Del Solar on cassette:
Y a nosotros nos toca, hoy, ponerte en libertad
tap-tap-tap, tap-tap!
How is it, now that you are free?
Abiding pain in your soul and heart
only chemically constructed euphoria
would imperfectly soothe.
Como está? now at rest from battle,
fought so valiantly with sword of pen or brush.
Your canvas leaning forever idle against a wall,
drawing book closed.
tap-tap-tap, tap-tap!
How is it, now that you don't have to see?
Things you saw so clearly through to their essence:
inequity
unrequited beauty
How does it feel, now that you can float above
let others do the work of coping,
resisting,
creating anew?
tap-tap-tap, tap-tap!
tap-tap-tap, tap-tap! *Buscando América*
And it's our turn today to set you free

Counting

My first real love
—not the puppy love of high school—
became my first real death
—different from my grandmother's passing—

and I had to really mourn and release,
before my own rebirth
—second (spiritual), after first (literal)—was possible.

Five years to say *goodbye*
and then turn to my own mortality.
Five years more before the seeds
of virus blossomed, *full blown*.

Ten years from onset of virus till
invention of (still imperfect) drugs to treat it.
One good friend, gone
before he could benefit
from better drugs that came too late.
Three that formed "the cocktail" combo.

Countless, the ways this virus
steered my path.
Unquantifiable,
the sadness for those
who left too early

Walking with the Wind

Walking with the wind today
all the Autumn leaves are in play,

whether shake-dancing on their branches,
or dry rustling on the ground.

Those once red, yellow, gold,
now browned,

mixing with pine needles in a brew
mapping out patterns best discerned

from above, by geese who flew by
on their way to southern spots.

A bit like the Haves, who leave behind
the Have Nots for warmer climes

when a chill sets in. Soon, those
havens will be gone. Luxury bungalow

playgrounds swallowed up by swells
and surges. Atlantis created

by consumerist urges.
Walking with the wind today

grey and white bands of cloud in play,
crisscrossing a pale blue sky, bright

with the telephone wires lit true,
glittering so beautifully in a spotlight,

displayed in their best light,
as only the sun's rays can do.

Caught by Chance

Pink in the sky! Lit by a rising sun.
Framed in bared branches' tentacles,
reaching up to touch soft, cotton-candy-
colored fluffs.

I look for shapes. A shark, it seems,
floating up in the sky. The color of a shell's interior,
rosy from morning's light. The blue he swims through,
true, like Caribbean waters, turquoise and clear.

This cloud-shark patrols lofty territory, cruising
through pink seagrasses, kelp, and algae,
camouflaged and completely at home.
Only vulnerable to a breeze, which will take

the outer edges of this mist-shark's shape along for a ride,
nudging form into some other creation, to loom,
hover, and glide. A changeable scene. Pink inhabitants
of a blue welkin sea, the reward of an upward glance.

Aquatic forms, caught by chance,
in a fleeting, cloud-ocean, gifted to us
down below,
on this beautiful, fluid morning.

Long Term Survival

If I were to throw a stone
and watch the ripples go back, back,
through waters of some thirty years,
there you'd be.

Back a little further, and there you'd be, stronger.
Still full of life's dramas; bursting with creativity.
No track marks mapping grief.
And I? Full-cheeked; rosy with naiveté.

Not yet ravaged by diseases preying on diminished immunity;
their treatments and their prevention.
Shaman now, conceding to ingestion of pills in a daily cluster,
I chant my spell of beseechment:

Take toxicity away; let there be harmony and balance in my being.

Surviving, feet are in both places, light, and dark.
Having met me in grisly proximity, mortality
rides along close, forever in the back pocket of life,
and I know each morning as a gift others never got to open.

Seed Sower

I gather myself into myself again,
I shall take my scattered selves and make them one

I shall collect them as seeds to sow,
and cultivate a garden there.
See what arises;
how they blossom and grow.
What stems appear; what leaves;
what petals, colors, scents.

I shall rejoice at the bounty, celebrate
riches of depth and variety;
texture, shape, maturity.
I will let a sense of peace; a serenity,
glow in me.

December Clear

When every leaf that's going to fall
is off its tree, when just the trunks stand tall,
and branches mark their lines in the sky;

when you can see through to any nests,
and see clear the view behind
and beyond every stand and thicket;

wind allowed to whistle between and around,
and no buffer for the barking dog
whose voice echoes through the yard,

across the road, to the other side of town.
No padding. No fluff. No mitigation.
Just stark and clear and true.

Leafless trees no *mincing of words,*
revealing the sky, showing
clustered clouds previously obscured.

These days feel like there's no running for shelter,
nowhere to hide. Ills festering un-cured.
Caught in a flashlight's beam, are things

in place as they're meant to be? Are we deer
stunned in the light, seeking moments of clarity?
Do our branches reach strong, offer a basket

widespread, sprigs woven with verity?
Like a scalp newly shorn, what is revealed?
Winter's sun lights lichen on bark, scarred and smooth.

Cold wind sings through crisscrossed
twigs' lace of open spaces,
narrating a ballad of the trees.

April Locket

for Jorge Soto Sanchez

Heart shaped, in my birthday month,
I keep the image of you.

April, so full of hope
for sun, and buds, and blossom.

I don't know the month we met. It was warm.
Summer time. An art exhibit space.

We shared our lives together at young love's accelerated pace.
You left. It was before the disease had a name

that was spoken aloud. Only whispered with fear and shame.
No cure; not even viable treatment back then.

Amazingly, I stayed alive. Watched others drown in that lake
of different fate. Survival/or not, a question worn daily, and
    handled

like prayer beads, draped around searching fingers.
Looking back into my locket at you,

sadness lingers. Here's April again; another birthday to mark.
I've a few grey hairs, everything and nothing to fear.

Grateful for blessings, I shed
a heart-shaped tear.

Remembering Jorge

Constant motion. Dot-dot-dot,
cross-hatch cross-hatch cross-hatch,

the scritch-scratch of pen on page.
You filled drawing books this way.

White pages turned herringbone and houndstooth
with shading and shaping.

Bodies, faces, places.
Hearts, phalluses, breasts.

Round bellies and buttocks,
cheekbones, third eyes.

Pain and love and nature and cityscape.
Moon, stars. Scars of childhood, loves of manhood.

You told your story on page after page,
stretched canvas and cardboard.

Your heart poured through your pen,
stroked canvases thick with gesso.

It bled and bled a crimson love
until it burst its seams and stopped.

Like a Ballet Star

It was Cade who invited you, Scott, to visit
the rural farm in VT, and help teach summer camp animation.

Different from life in Chicago where you strutted the city.
So vibrant and pretty; we met when you were a beautiful guest

in my dance class. Pointing your feet like a ballet star;
doing Martha Graham contraction and release long-legged,

strong. You took to center stage with uninhibited energy.
No one would have guessed, in those days, you had HIV.

But time took its toll. Back home in Chicago, in the care
of loving boyfriend, you put your young house in order.

Cashed in your life insurance; splurged on a Jeep with leather
    seats;
an end-of-life car. You weren't going to reach mid-life crisis;
    never

going to get that far. Live all bells and whistles now; nothing
    cheap.
Time to live it up; be in the moment; pamper yourself.

But, a moment came when, at twenty-something, death inescapable
shook you, with a predatory disease of the lungs.

So grateful I'd traveled west and we had that day,
visiting the Art Institute; sat out on blankets at night,

a concert in the park (was it Mozart) letting the light
of stars fill us, before Aspergillus took you,

my wonderful friend,
away.

A Poet I Know

for Dean Rhetoric

A poet I know on Twitter
said he's "poet laureate of Tesco meal deals."

Well, I've never heard of those,
but I get what he means.

I replied, "poet laureate of birdfeeder watchers."
Because, I am. Self-appointed.

I get that we both have known loneliness.
Not the *missing people you like to hang out*

with kind, but the *spend most of your time alone,
with yourself, for years* kind.

Not sure about his, but mine was imposed
by major illness and the stigma that came

with it. People were afraid.
Death was all but certain.

That was a long time ago.
Now, it's managed.

I'm good at watching birds. I'm getting
somewhat good at writing about it.

I'm glad that, whatever Dean's story is,
he's writing about it too.

Laura's Lights

Shadows meander across a wall;
footprint tracks follow her in snow.
Though hesitant to read what's been
written as response to the prompt,
I think she wants us to know.
The one in our group most like a painter,
Laura's words sketch sights, sounds, emotions.
The strong presence of her cat. Memories, colors,
scenarios. Impressions in ink marking a page.

Tonight she tells us she's feeling able to turn
her apartment lights on. She hadn't been, for fear
of being seen. Coming out of darkness, Laura explains,
It's different; it changes things. Seems not all shadows
were benevolent strokes in motion across her wall.
Not all presence simpatico as her cat.
Recovered memories traverse through time. Gradually,
she dares to share. *I'm starting to feel safe enough*. We listen
together in a circle; and we care.

Provincetown Night

Moon over rooftop,
under tree branch leaves,
colors our evening
clouds.

Pallet of grays, blue, white.
Green crowns tickle the edges,
raised by old-world trunks barking
chimney level high.

Watch as the day's sky transforms
to night.
Bay close; its harbored
boats big and small.

Ocean on the other side, stretched
long, with sandy shore.
Shark-flag flutters announce
underwater presence

near this thin, hook-shaped curve
of land,
home to flowers abundant,
butterflies and birds.

Patio balcony metal chair painted white
displays tide-gifted rocks and shells.
Sun-bleached cedar shingles everywhere
line narrow alleyways

to the anywheres
in our mind.

Colored Birds Bouquet

a Coexistence Triolet

Birds come to the feeder, colored like a luscious bouquet of flowers.
Awareness that we share this planet making me so buoyantly happy.
Their feather-petals yellow, blue, the red of sky in evening hours.
Birds at the feeder blossoming like a luscious bouquet of flowers.
These sweet little creatures' presence wielding incredible powers to elicit empathy, wonder, fascination; emotions strong as nectar is sappy.
Multicolored birds visit our feeder like a luscious gift bouquet of flowers.
Awareness of our precious synchrony making me fly-away-happy!

What Is Freedom?

Seed party!
Little birds have discovered them
in our blue coffee-pot feeder

They cling to its mesh and feast
on the black oil sunflower seeds
flit, flit

swoop, swoop
back and forth branch to feeder
to branch . . .

Such happiness outside my November window
with the leaves down
and cold winds blowing in

"Let It Be" comes on the radio
and I sing out
with tears in my eyes

Marie Yovanovitch's* red hair
from last night's TV
matches the breast of a small bird.

* Former United States Ambassador to Ukraine (2016–2019)

Ovine

We sheep.
Your wool so good against mine.
Close together, moving as a clump;
warm breath, spongy thick-coats. Followers.
A flock of followers; we clomp where directed.
A herd.

Have you heard? Our group is being trimmed.
Those at the periphery. The un-able, unstable ones
pushed to the outside, sheared off to the wayside.

Our directors do this. With their dogs, they keep us
moving grazing feeding, clumping.
They grow fat. Our group is thinned. Groomed.
And we don't even know; don't notice at all.
We just keep moving. Grazing, feeding, sleeping.

Practice

As the household sleeps,
in this morning's golden dawn,

I practice qigong. Exercises
shifting weight, shifting breath,

making circles with arms, hips,
eventually coming to moves

named for bear, eagle, lion, crane.
Blood is pumping, but my soul is still.

In movement, but calm, I float
in space, not concentrating anymore

on potential tragedy; anxiety.
Our family, extended family, the world,

seem under shadows. This changes, or
does not change, but I have spread the mountains

with my arms; I can flex and flow,
come what may. Maybe, for now.

Wild Bindweed, Yarrow, and Me

Ubiquitous bindweed;
glowing white flowers flash
at me from verge and meadow.

Attention-getters, indeed.
Their modest and constant neighbor:
yarrow.

Yarrow, yarrow,
a delicate flower;
many small blossoms

held on its tall slim stem,
possessing a quiet power
to dance with the breeze.

Yarrow, yarrow
meet me tomorrow;
same time, same place.

Rooted strong,
reaching proud,
upright, with grace.

I pledge to stand alongside;
to notice and honor you,
existing in joy, or sorrow.

Yarrow, yarrow, people my dreams
of yesterday; color this
present moment's hopes.

Let's find place alongside
bindweed's strobing ambitions
to flourish tomorrow.

Glass Half-Full Today

On my favorite morning,
I'm sitting near the window

where outside hangs a simple feeder
for the birds. Mostly smaller ones

who can pull black oil sunflower seeds
through the mesh of this painted blue

metal coffee pot shape. They come and go,
come and go, taking turns swooping in,

and off again. It's early February; a fresh
NewEngland snowfall covers the recent brown-and-exposed.

Light grows stronger, lasts longer. We're marching
toward votes and valentines. Ready to turn from darkness,

could there be a chance of meaningful change
in the air? On this favorite morning, I am singing

aloud, to the radio, whose station "gets me."
Beautiful voices; beautiful words

and I sing along with them, feeling the vibration
in my heart. All of a sudden a small bird, different

from the black-capped, white-cheeked little chickadees,
settles on the birdfeeder mesh, and lingers awhile.

Touched by the extraordinary sight
of its tomato-red breast under mud-brown wings,

I sing, *Hello lovely! Thank you for appearing.*
Welcome to my favorite morning.

Wash and Overlay

As evening approaches,
sun sets behind branches
who leave tangled patterns
in the sky.

This unruly-snarl, like hair
pulled from a brush, a free-form mandala
whose intricate shapes generate outward,
one from another.

Each branch-line a dark silhouette
against white and blue-grey. Brush-stroked
faded denim watercolor wash,
with India ink overlay.

My very own cathedral-glass design
of light through shape. Reminding:
take an in-breath, and out, serene.
Shimmering connections, revealed

to all who look anew. Take comfort
in gifts given, everywhere. Be amazed
at spiderweb's silver cape, glinting,
bejeweled, in rainbowed dots of dew.

As the Spring Birds Sing

Coronavirus Diary XII
4/13/2020

As birds sing of spring,
we sit in sorrow.
Under pandemic lockdown, not sure
of our tomorrow,
jobs and livelihood disappear.
Hunkered down in required isolation,
each day, we're losing ones held dear;
uncles, teachers, grocery store workers.
Grandparents sealed in their eldercare homes
wave to family through locked doors and windows.
As we shelter within our enclosing walls,
red foxes roam; hedgehogs wander.
Left to usher in spring without human hustle
and bustle, Earth catches her breath.
We hide behind masks; scramble for ventilators,
as birds build nests in the branches and bramble.
This year, crowded hospital beds groan
as lilac boughs bud, preparing to blossom.

Coronavirus Diary

3/14/2020

*I dreamt I woke up, and Covid-19 was a dream
not a disaster.
It had never happened, and things were the same.*

Covid-19 and I'm grinding my teeth again.
Broken bloody teeth enter my dreams.
As well as a niece who's sick and knows it,
yet comes too near.
Weaponized coughing. Sneezes of death.

I've come to resent the closeness
of my husband's breath, misting our pillow.
Shelves now stocked with extra
peanut butter, soap, and sprays. In case
there's a shortage, or the demand to stay in.

Through the late 80s and 90s, I survived
a virus for which there is no cure.
Left a swath of death in its wake.
Changed the course of many lives, forever.
I lived, have two kids, and grow old;

am good at "being in the moment."
I appreciate small and beautiful things.
But these days of darkening news, anxiety builds
like a Hitchcockian thriller, highlighting
all we have to lose.

In the Silence

In the silence of tall-treed woods,
I hear the acorns falling.

On paved road, they crack and pop
under my feet.

Pale purple asters bloom as scruffy
star shaped bursts.

Fire-red vines grow alongside, licking
verge edges; spiraling around tree trunks.

Sumac leaf feathers dipped in red
like arrow tips of a bloody hunt.

Somewhere in the 1970s, we took a wrong turn,
followed an erroneous path into the 1980s,

slept too long, and now, how we wail.
We fall to our knees and keen at the loss of so many

birds and trees. We choke on waste piles
of mistake; drown in high water of short sight;

roast in flames of shame, as blinders rip off
and join a floating garbage vortex shadowing

bleached coral reefs.
When I hear a bird call high above, I wake.

Make sure to crane my neck, raise my gaze,
notice, locate, love.

Before, and After

Coronavirus Diary VI
3/25/2020

Dry cough . . . and I worry.
Slight headache lingers . . .

is this the end?
Shortened temper; I'm annoyed

with my 85-year-old mother for hovering
as I do requested tasks.

The mother who took me back in;
sheltered me in the darkest days

of my progression from HIV to AIDS.
That was the 80s.

Now, she's in her 80s, I've been "undetectable"
for years, and she needs my help.

I worry at night for my own kids.
One, living in a current "hot spot"

for Covid-19. The other, still a teenager,
handed an abrupt end to his college

experience, started and adjusted to
only a few months ago.

But, that was all BEFORE,
and now, we are in the midst of AFTER.

Who will crawl through the tunnel
and make it to the other side?

What will greet them there?

Coronavirus Diary II

3/16/2020

Congregating (in groups more than fifty)
has become a danger.
Especially for those over sixty.
In the Covid-19 pandemic,
we are sitting ducks.
My Father, sealed into his elder-care home.
Our younger son and college mates could be carriers.
This sucks!
Fear is creating toilet paper hoarders;
hand-sanitizer hogs.

A large group of crows is called "a murder."
It seems we are all just swirling
black dots on a cluster graph,
mapping out contagion.
However, some communities
are forming; becoming stronger.
Books-to-read lists are circulating;
poems exchanged.
I was sent a link to "sixty minutes of calming music."
Yes. Music is magic.

Humming, still alive, I'll hold tight
to hope that Spring flowers arrive.

Descending on Us All

Coronavirus Diary VII
3/25/2020

There is a desperate friendliness
in the smile from walkers

as we separate to either side
of the street or sidewalk,

passersby in a pandemic.
The grin is a little too wide

the lips pulled to an almost-grimace,
calling to mind skeletons—

the just skull and bones we are—
beneath it all. This is a friendliness desperate

to show connection. The distancing,
desperate to avoid droplets of a breath

which could be virus-laden,
in a time of isolation and sequestering

into private bubbles of protection,
hoping to avoid a sweeping coronavirus

cloud as it descends
on us all.

Wild Goats of Llandudno *Lockdown*

Coronavirus Diary IX
4/2/2020

Go goats, go!
Run wild, run free!

munch the hedges,
run atop ledges,

swarm the streets.
Stick together, or stray apart,

there's no one to stop you now.
We're at a distance,

sequestered in our bubbles,
living by remote.

How amazing to be a goat just now
and not hold back!

Feel your power; feel the wind
in your fleece!

Fly, fly through our streets
like a squadron of migrating geese!

We watch from windows, capture
you on video,

share with our captive kind,
through clouds of internet,

as we dream of freedom.

Re-Traumatized

Thank you, John Prine, "Angel from Montgomery"

Make me a cardinal
who flies to the pine boughs.

Give me a good song
from the old radio.

Chirp to me
like a black-capped chickadee;

just pierce my heart
and I'm down on my knees.

Well, the snow is melting,
and the wind is howling,

and everyone around me
is feeling ill today.

I've survived one epidemic,
found love, and had children,

but the coming pandemic
is getting me re-traumatized.

Make me a cardinal who flies
to the pine bough.

Sneeze into your elbow
and don't come this way.

I don't know the remedy
to keep on surviving.

I don't have the answers;
just keep living day by day.

Woman Under Covid-19

Coronavirus Diary VIII
3/27/2020

Caretaker; nurturer;
these are underlying traits.

Building a nest; incubating eggs.
Gathering and preparing food

to drop in gaping, wanting,
upturned mouths. Providing comfort,

sustenance, encouragement,
survival.

It's a world on one's shoulders,
carried with grace.

But under pandemic all is shifted.
Coronavirus re-calibrates powers of sacrifice.

How can I possibly do enough
to save children? husband? parents?

If breath is stolen, and we struggle,
my heart may break, striving to breathe for two.

Coronavirus Diary V

3/24/2020
The Elms

A first death from Covid-19 in our state.
NH is small, but it's connected to VT,
which connects to NY, the current
pandemic "hot spot" of the east coast.
Where our older son now lives.
NYC is where he's been able
to thrive. Will he survive?

Before this is over, everybody will know
a family member, friend, or acquaintance
who was taken. Just like with AIDS.
They called it *the gay virus* early on,
until it started non-discriminating.
Hemophiliacs, IV drug users, actors, models,
artists, musicians. Scientists, doctors, teachers,
uncles, grandmothers, brothers. Whole swaths
of people gone.
Currently, the American President insists
on the name *Chinese virus* for our pandemic.

I remember *Dutch Elm Disease*.
Growing up in the 70s, I saw it take the trees.
In our Ivy League NH town, Wheelock St. was lined
with regal Elms, arching across the road,
forming a chuppah of branches overhead.
One by one they became diseased and cut down.
Replaced by Maple, or Oak, which would eventually,
over years, grow tall—but never the same.

Coronavirus Diary III

3/20/2020

It's not as though life is perfect
and everything is shining and smooth.

No, there's a lot I'm unsatisfied with.
Many cluttered things, undone, in dust.

So why is there this precious feeling
like an ache in my heart

when the birds sing?
They sing, and fly together,

in the breeze
and the branches

and my heart cracks open
like the ice cliffs calving.

And the thought that life may end
is an unbearable thing.

Coronavirus Diary IV

3/23/2020

The odor of yeast bubbling
in warm honey sweetness

as my husband starts his bread.
It sits in a large ceramic bowl, covered

with damp thin cotton tea-towel,
waiting to get punched down

at the appropriate time.
Meanwhile, we do our qigong exercises

in front of the desk-top, as a white clad
practitioner we have stored in the cloud

does his slow moves with names tagging
crane, lion, bear. *Expand the chest*

to cleanse the body. Eagle spreads its wings
and bear swims across the water.

Our son, sequestered in a bedroom
of his childhood, has been robbed

of the experience, new for him last Fall,
of being on college campus, learning

about life, with his peers.
Instead, they must practice *social distancing,*

and attend *virtual learning* classes
on Zoom.

Arctic Breezes in May

Coronavirus Diary XV
5/13/20

Arctic breezes blow through this May,
even on a sunny day, as pipe-smoke clouds float
in blue sky and songbirds illuminate the Spring.

Cold winds bleat, ominous,
telling us, *Not safe to relax.*
Human activity forced to slow, Earth takes a pause now.
A prolonged in-breath, where we can notice
birds abundant and close-by. Cityscapes emerging
through lessened haze. Wild goats encroaching
on manicured hedges, having fun.

In this suspended time, let us consider
what's been done.
We un-stranded a sustaining weave.
Unraveled braids, one by one.
Flying threads now whip, wild
at the mercy of avenging winds.

How to breathe out again; take hold,
bind back parts entwined strong?
With lighter touch; inclusive, branching,
like mycelia, creating connections, we could
be integrated with Earth's fabric. In partnership,
we could be celebratory beads, sewn into a cosmos,
twinkling.

Shout

the Summer of 2020

Our pandemic history
flows from manic making
of banana breads, and no t.p.,
to where mass protest is urgent necessity.
A black man died under blue clad weight;
neck held down, casually,
by the racist knee of a bully cop
leaning into white supremacy,
brutalizing with impunity,
thinking his perceived racial superiority
grants him immunity;
permits him to act as vigilante.

Unrest and protest follows. Tsunami
amassing; a wave led by the outraged
brave building a roar to implement change,
correct wrongs; imagine more.
Imagine better and bring it about;
that is what people in the streets are calling for.
That is why we all must shout.

Only Love Songs

From now on, every poem I write
shall be simply
a love song.
Closing my eyes
because the planet is dying.
I must sing its beauty.
Closing my eyes because people
are trying for breath;
in a white supremacist grip.
And breath is peace. Breath is ease.
May we stop policing BREATH, please?!

From now on, I'll sing only of love;
write words of description;
petals, leaves, clouds, trees, hoping
We Shall Overcome. Peace, please
find us all on this overheating planet.
With the benevolent beauty
of a cooling breeze justice must prevail.
March in throngs, in a rainbow arch,
write the wrongs, chant the songs.

When the Pandemic Is Over

There will be something else.
Pessimistic, I know . . .
but, will the Planet even be living?
Will it be nurturing home to a species
who've abused and disrespected it so?

When the pandemic ends, I will hug
my father who's been sealed up
into the pod of his elder care home.
I will dance and sing, wave feathers,
light a smudge stick.
I will feel good for my son who's still trying
to have college experience.
And my other son who's been working "remotely."

When the pandemic ends when it ends
Will it end?
Will there be another, different virus?
Will we have killed off all underprivileged
and underserved, leaving only
previously pampered survivors?

When the pandemic ends, I will pick a bouquet
and smell the flowers.
I will drink pure clear water and wade
at the meeting of sand and surf on a beach
where there are only shells and no plastics
strewn or oil surfacing in footprints.

When the pandemic ends
we'll sit around a campfire
and tell our tales. We will remember the lost;
the dead and damaged.

When the pandemic ends, will I have learned
something? Anything?
There will be TV shows, plays and books
about it. We have to tell our stories.

When the pandemic ends
ends
ends.
Fingertips will touch another
and really feel
feel
the surface of a skin
that isn't our own.

When the pandemic ends
clean air will be valued.
Breathing will be sacred.
We will build statues to our lungs.
The shape of lungs, like a heart.

Breath. Breathing.
Feeling. Seeing.
When the pandemic ends.

Connection

for Max-Henry
after You Are Everything, *REM 1988*

Sometimes it feels I will never sleep
dark, dark is the night
Afraid of the world; the world we've made
dark is the night

Afraid of disconnection. Imagine riding
in a car; try to imagine—there is no internet!
The windows surround you
and point out the stars

Press your face to the glass
gaze out at the sky. It's vast
and winking; spilling
with sparkles twinkling

You're moving through space
white lines shoot by; a rhythm
to the night. Secure in this vessel
driven by others, you trust in the future . . .

Sometimes it feels I will never sleep
dark, dark is the night
Afraid of this world that we've made
dark, dark is the night

Go back to a sense of wonder *Try* look out
at the birds in your tree, *living*
outside of your window
they're there for you to see. *Why?*

Put down, put down the phone. Use binoculars.
Yellow wings match perfectly the changing leaves.
See this blending has a purpose;
puzzle pieces nestle into their places

Before It Goes, Remember

Remember when you could sleep
at the end of day, with expectation
that upon rise,
our world would be okay

When you felt a sense
of balance under your feet;
connection to earth and sky
Because they were alive

and well. And you could tell that
from abundance. Birds in the air,
flowers in the field, bees in the hive
Remember

when clouds were clouds
and not hovering doom
foretelling fire storms, flood,
Polar ice ablation

Remember when you felt we were marching
toward Justice
maybe too slowly but at least
in that direction

When you believed
in election
being fair and true representation
without question.

Red

The euonymus are flaming.
Their little feather leaves, red
as coxcomb and wattle
on a rooster's head.
Red standing out from the rest,
like the wheelbarrow (in that poem)
so much depends upon.
Each bush a fireball of heat
set aflame by October. A last-blast
celebration before winter's wan.
Take notice, Red says. *Take heed.*
Gather all you need; shore up.
What's ahead can be harsh.
Gather wood now,
so together, we may sit,
rosy, at the fire.

11/7/2020

City people dancing in the streets
exorcising built-up toxicity

Here, amongst tall trees,
recently bared, I've
made a celebration cake.
confetti colored sprinkles
on a white frosting cloud
atop dark cocoa sponge.

Something had to be done
to codify the joy
the relief an out-breath
before our struggles resume.

From AIDS to Covid

In the eighties, we met. We loved.
Before the nineties, you were gone.
Didn't get to live into your forties.

And I knew, from my late twenties on,
I'd be living with, and likely dying
from the AIDS virus too.

Though this fate would own me,
turns out I was luckier than you.
Meds improved. T-cells could climb

into the hundreds (seven was my low).
Full of pharmaceuticals and their sculpting,
experiencing the valleys of alienation,

still holding your drawings, paintings,
and the memories . . .
I've now made it through all of my fifties.

I've a husband, children, house with apple tree
and view of a river . . . life flows on.
But, facing this new virus, Covid,

there's some PTSD. Memory of the pain
all those years ago; fears and battles
first faced by you, then me.

Since the Epidemic

In the early years of my survival,
I kept a downward gaze
not wanting to be seen
not wanting to have to explain.

It took joining instagram to bring
my eyes up and raise my look out.
I started to see things; details
in everyday places.

I catalogued rust, paint peeling,
bricks, and graffiti; dried leaves
on old drain grates. And I started sharing.
Posting with hashtags, winning best picture

contests for doors, wabi-sabi walls
or lost abandoned toys. The outward gaze
helped me be more comfortable in a world
where I'd lost my place.

Eventually, it was poetry I would find
as language and space to tell the story
of who I am; my journey forward,
memories back.

Nuyorican in Vermont

Tyehimba Jess, the poet, posts
a tweet today; a video
of Miguel Algarín (just passed away).
Long live the spirit of the Nuyorican . . .
Pouring one out Jess says.
The video shows compañeros pouring drink
on the street; they toast, laugh, recite.
It takes me back some thirty-seven years,
to you. *We pour a little on the sidewalk*
for the boys inside you said, explaining
this ritual of remembrance; respect.
To know someone in jail was as foreign for me
as the island of Puerto Rico, where we visited
your Aunt's house in Bayamón, art galleries
in Old San Juan, rock formations at the shore.
It was around 1984.
You still lived in El Barrio (was it East 103rd?)
in your studio. Artwork covered every wall.
A long canvas held in-process figures;
life-sized, created in texture and gesture;
motion and emotion; the thick gesso-acrylic mix
holding your strokes, your struggles and strengths,
visible in whites and blues, hints of red.
In Vermont, you painted too. *The mountains*
remind me of Puerto Rico, you said,
telling me of visits there in your youth; respite
from harsh edges in Nuevo York.
Hearing news of his death, you drew a loving portrait
of Gilberto, last seen in NYC gaunt, with a cane;
haunted, frightened of the virus in his veins.
Were you frightened too?
It was before you got so sick.
Walks past corn fields labored. Eventually bedded
with pneumonia (Pneumocystis; the opportunistic one).

Always, you drew and drew. Mountains, figures, faces,
a bird leaving someone's mouth like breath, the moon.
Death took you away from us Jorge.
Cruelly, and too soon. Death found you
like so many others you'd known,
and those I'd yet to meet.

What Are Some Other Side Effects of This Drug?

Two in the morning
I hear the wall clock ticking.

Pacing, I know stars are out,
hanging low in the sky.

Padding trips to the bathroom,
peeking out our window into the dark.

Wee hours twitter scrolling
both reassures and depresses.

Strengthens my sense of connection,
but also how we are all so doomed.

Gleaned like looking in a funhouse mirror;
a comic strip where evil wins the day,

corruption and greed seem
to have gained an upper hand.

Maybe downward dog stretch
will help, and bring me into dawn.

Ars Poetica

Not pulled to drawing (like you; always with
blank book, filling in every inch of each page,
ink constantly flowing),

I sketch the pad with words from a pen,
and tap-tap the keyboard keys with finger tips.
Writing is a language I am cultivating

after your death and my long journey
with disease. All those silent years processing
pain of loss and reckoning with prognosis

of death—grisly death—at thirtysomething
(which was ten years down the road). Well,
I am decades past that, full of pills, and I need

to speak now. I am shading it all in.
Not so much to tell, but to figure out.
To claim. To uncover an identity.

COMPROMISE/D

As though they strapped a pelt
of fat to my torso
like medieval armor
a plate placed over vital organs;
a stylized indentation indicates bellybutton.
A covering, like an armadillo's. Or like kangaroo,
or hoody, whose pouch is stuffed full
so that, weighted down, it hangs
low, pulled by gravity. Hangs over
twice-marked line of cesarean sections.

Virus-stopping medicine places these pelts
of fat on my upper arms like pudding;
like padding for a rough and tumble game;
maybe to repel a fast-moving puck.
There's a mound on my back now too,
just at the neck.

All these alterations add up to not owning
this body-dwelling anymore.
Not ME, this mal-shaped form!
ME remains underneath, a naive
twenty-year-old, wondering *how did I get here*
Do I live now in a costume . . . forever?

I'll take the pills; wear the coat of survival,
but will never concede that its imposed form
exhibits who I am beneath.

M.O. the Poet

Marihew Oman stands
at the podium. Poet.
Round head weighty.
Face an uncut pie;
a necco wafer disk;
a full harvest moon.

Speaking with power,
intensity, voice projecting electric
sincerity, gentle sensitivity
unmasked in words
disclosing an open heart
worn on the sleeve.
No mush or wishy wash;
sharp and to the point,
a hunter for truth,

Marihew throws a spear
piercing our comfort zone;
brings us out to the open field
of possibility, and there,
offers an invitation
for change.

We Hunt for Mercy

A suit of wings may be what's needed, to soar
above it all, though we've Icarus' example as warning.
From this suit of wings, no wax will melt,
no hubris bring a fall. We'll stay within
reasonable realm, just high enough
to skim the fires, the floods, the locust swarms,
angry plagues of retribution. Perchance,
above carbon clouds of dread, we'll see solution,
receive survival vision. Perhaps
a topographical map of how
to save us. With rainbow wings,
searching contour lines,
our flight buoyed by the spirit
of regal feathered birds who glide
on winds of hope, we hunt
for mercy.

Another Chickadee Poem

All pandemic long, I've been watching
chickadees.

Observing their swooping flight
to the feeder from scraggly branches.

Always taking turns;
no collisions, no fights.

Swoop in, take a seed,
swoop out.

I could watch them all day,
like flame of a campfire

or a baby in a crib, looking up
with sparkling eyes, existing

in some joyful world where knowledge
of hateful things hasn't entered.

That shining pool
of innocence.

The irises like doors
to infinity

inviting you
back in.

Winter of My Sixtieth Year

As it turns out,
I am aged now!
With wrinkles my grandmother once wore.
Like foil that was scrunched
into a fist, then opened,
to lay on bones as a face.

As it turns out, Grandma is long gone,
her daughter is now the old one
and the kind one,
holding the family together
with her care.

As it turns out, I don't feel the wisdom
that you'd assume comes with wrinkles.
I feel instead, sometimes, clueless;
helpless; uncertain.
Was Grandma's focus on collecting
beautiful teacups and rings a way to escape?

As it turns out, there's a need to escape
the looming dread
of an uncertain future
for our children's world.
One we'll be leaving behind.

That Which Makes Us Joyful

A blue horse turns into a streak of lightning,
*   then the sun—*
relating the difference between sadness
*   and the need to praise*
that which makes us joyful.
                    —Joy Harjo, "Promise of Blue Horses"

Birds embody the shapes of my heart
these days

holding the warmth of a hug
in their feathers

the gleam of a kiss in
their eyes

building a home for my love
in their beaks

and spreading, with their song,
the promise of blue horses.

Wishing Well

I threw another stone to
the wishing well today.

A small splash,
but a splash none the less.

It will hit the water
and ripples will radiate

to the edges of that well.
The stone will join others

thrown with intention
and hope.

Today I will focus on the throwing;
the rippling; the intention.

I will find strength in the fact
that I am not alone

taking this action.
The arc of Justice is long

but acts of faith are relentless; strong.
Relentless.

Strong.
Relentless.
Strong.

Turn the Corner

Goodbye 2020. I've eaten my fill
of snickerdoodles, gingerbread,
chocolate chip cookies, yeast bread ladened
with dates, butter, brown sugar. Sweetness

and goo enough to bring me down
the last lap; the exhausting
strangely disconnected limbo
of *end-of-the-year*.

This particular year had a harsh coating
of *pandemic* gloating in our faces like shiny egg wash,
painted on with threat of death; wreaking
of sorrow and loss, tragedy and cruelty. Separation.

Thankful for the birds-a-plenty, green pine, storybook snow,
warmth and food enough. Being able to behold young love,
and muddle through old. To see the bright moon dazzling
in night's sky. Enjoy our elders being amongst us.

I snap these pictures, in my mind; the lovely moments.
Shoring up, storing them in heart and memory,
stacked like sand bags against storm waters rising;
a hope for resiliency.

A Large Bear Swims

The shadow shape in front of me looks almost
normal, walking afternoon roads.

Arms, almost shapely. Body, almost
proportional.

None of that pear-shaped loping;
this seems almost a jaunt.

My seventy-dollar haircut—an almost unheard of event—
might be doing the trick.

This looks like the shadow of a Real Person
with a Real Life.

None of that existing on the edges, in the verges,
out of mainstream's flow.

Must be just the right angle
for sun meeting grey outline

to create this illusion of "good shape."
I'll take it; I'll take the encouragement.

Large bears can swim through water.
Heavy, wet-coated bodies can be buoyant

and move forward.

Insomnia Song

Sleep, come to me.
I long for your embrace.
To wake in the morning, refreshed;
ready to face the seasons, come what may.

Sleep, come to me.
I'll ride your rolling waves to shore,
lapping sand, rocks, shells,
salty and bleached from the sun.

Sleep, come to me.
Let me float in your clouds'
morphing form;
a white pillowy mist.

Sleep come to me,
and we will see what tolls are paid
to enter a highway of dreams.

Sleep, gentle sleep, I breathe you in,
and out.
I ride you up,
and down.
My pulse has slowed; my frown is gone.
Be my guardian.

Gently Let This Day

after "Let This Day" by Annie Lighthart, Pax *(Fernwood Press, 2021)*

Let this day born in aches and pains
change. Let it stretch and bend,
downward-dogging into an elongated
relaxation where breath brings
renewal and strength, and an ability
to view all from underneath, upside down,
and eventually, gently, with a twist,
skyward.
Now see how the birds sing together,
perched high on branches in the strong sun.
Black feather bodies catching each ray
and offering back a rainbow glisten. Watch,
relax, reflect, listen!

Solace

Snubbed by it, I understand the value of sleep
so well just now.

The velvety comfort of it. Waking refreshed, clear,
renewed. *You don't know what you've got till*

it's gone. Yes, indeed, Joni Mitchell. You called it;
and so young.

I will go to music, whenever possible, for solace.
Wrap it around me like a quilt;

relax into the warmth. Let a good ballad grab hold
and melt like campfire marshmallows sliding

down their stick. A voice skewered with aching
lyrics over a jangly bare-boned tune stabs

the target every time, and takes me away
to a place I can rest.

There, I'll sit in the lap of well-sung struggle;
ache; emotion; longing,

let it all bleed out,
and lay my burden down.

Arise

Swimming through dirt,
I reach for you.

Like a mink in water,
cutting through dark current,

forcing aside grains of earth,
following the smell of you;

tracking the vibration of you.
We will unite and rise together

having fed on droplets and loam.
Nourished, entwined,

it's only sunshine we seek.
Petals to wind, like palms

cupped. Let's sing our song
for this season.

Moon, Deer, Mountains, Stars

When moon masquerades
as a whisp of cloud . . . hiding
in plain sight, shying
from earth's troubled faces, avoiding
that walker below, whose eyes pry, searching
heights for escape . . . or signs of hope

and a young deer appears at sidewalk edge
—gazes lock; walker, deer—frozen in a moment
of recognition. A flick of white as, in flight,
cloven tracks disappear into a scrim of nearby trees,
whose leaves flutter the sigh of release.

Walk and walk now, upright one, until skies purple
with dusk, mountains blue on distant horizon; vessels
afloat in darkening tide. Stars line up for tonight's debut
. . . set to twinkle like pin heads pushed into pooled ink,
sparkling silver, as soon as night's curtain rises.

Every Small Breeze

Pie-top shapes rest on walls I pass; porch-chair shadows
cast by latticed metalwork in morning's sun

As air conditioners whirr, mimicking sounds of Ocean,
they're missing a rhythm of the waves

As treetops breathe in floating clouds and little birds
sing, nestled, sheltered by feathered leaves

As mother and daughter pick blueberries
in the distance, across a lime-green field

As milkweed, bindweed, and tall grasses mingling
host a butterfly, who decorates in flits and flutters

As wild carrot flowers spangle with blossom-galaxies
waving atop tall stems, and vine leaves burst into pinwheels of
    green

As a long-fallen log rests, glistening its bright
mottled-white birchbark, peeling in the sun

As I mop beading sweat from hat-brimmed brow
before it can trickle a salty stream to my eyes

As every small breeze becomes sacred
and each breath a gift, I walk in steps

As I will do tomorrow and tomorrow,
as long as I am able.

Sweet Things

Upright and tight fisted.
Poised to release.
Each pink peony bud,
potential enclosed;
vitality condensed.

In June, solstice coming,
each will open, spill forth
beauty and fragrance
like fireworks;
bright booming blooms.

Then, weighty petals
flutter down pooling
on garden ground;
stems arching
in summer's night,
making way for the next
sweet thing.

The heart is not

a trash bin
containing everything
that's been discarded.
No, it is instead a sieve, filtering
dust, rain, and sunbeams alike.
Glitter and song; fog, sleet,
and rainbows.
The heart is a gill, taking in
what comes,
trying to extract
what feeds us, and
let go what doesn't.

When blue breaks

through the clouds
in pools of relief

from solid monotone
grey-white kapok skies,

my heart sighs, rejoicing;
celebrating reprieve.

Oppressive grey covered all
like a silencer, muffling.

Blue breaking through
brings a melody

of gratitude.
A feeling that yes,

what's essential and true
presents itself

clear; crystal;
beyond hazy daze

cottony cover-up.
Blue breaks through,

sharp as thorn jutting
from a vine,

blue as a fallen icicle
piercing through snow.

Its shadow lands,
laying an arrow sign,

freeing possibility,
cracking open a lane for discovery

of what to do.

In a Riparian Zone

In this season, the river is revealed to us
through bared branches, through our back windowpanes,
its fog-steam rising in cold morning.
A brick smokestack's refracted reflection floats on its surface.
Once spewing toxins from a dry-cleaning facility,
the tall stack now stands dormant, still-reaching to clouds,
a vanishing point in our view to the west. How wide is the riparian
 band?
Does it have an end?
Looking out just now, I catch sight of two small flickers—
small black and white woodpeckers, one redheaded.
Then, the swoop-flight of wind-surfing black-capped chickadees
riding a current from tree to feeder-seeds, sending a thrill that
 rivers
over me and spreads, in ripples, to eternity.

Head in the Clouds

The cloud, so distant from me here,
on earth, on this wood of our deck,
on two feet, looking up.
I reel it in, and imagine
droplets misting my face . . .
tears or shower; relief, renewal;
its all there, in a white fluffy ball
changing semblance in winds
that come from all directions.
Able to morph, adapt.
Can I be the cloud? May I
take it as my cotton-filled pillow,
tuck it under my head,
let muscles relax,
and dream-visions come?
I send thoughts up and away.
Near, and far; supportive, and sieve-like,
I will bring cloud down, wrap it round,
wear it as a shawl, or skirt. I will twirl,
letting cloud take what shapes it may.
I know there are days I laugh aloud,
and in some, feel enveloped by trepidation.
Let me remember, while still free from shroud,
to lift my gaze and not ignore.
In that space and time, of each given day,
whichever season, let me adore,
adore, adore.

Notes

The poem "Fields and Verges" came from doing a prompted writing exercise in John Murillo's FAWC week-long workshop in August 2021. Much gratitude to them, and to other poets and workshops who make it possible to attend with generous scholarships, keeping inspiration, encouragement, and a sense of poetry community alive during the isolation of the pandemic.

The poem "Me" was used as part of the text of *Voices of the Silenced* (2019), an original work for chorus, piano, and strings by Norwegian composer Kim André Arnesen, commissioned by New Hampshire Master Chorale and performed in November 2019.

In the poem "Set You Free" lyrics quoted are from the song Buscando América, from Rubén Blades and Seis del Solar's first album, released April 3, 1984.

The first two lines in the poem "Seed Sower" are from *The Crystal Gazer* by Sara Teasdale (1884–1933).

Marie Yovanovitch, referred to in the poem "What Is Freedom?" was the United States ambassador to Ukraine from 2016–2019. She captivated the nation with her testimony before the House Intelligence Committee on November 15, 2019, in the first impeachment hearing of then-president Donald Trump.

The poem "Connection" is inspired by the song "You Are the Everything," written by Bill Berry, Peter Buck, Mike Mills, and Michael Stipe, which appears on *Green*, the sixth studio album by the band R.E.M., released on November 7, 1988.

The poem referred to as "that poem" in the poem "Red" is "The Red Wheelbarrow" by William Carlos Williams (1883–1963), originally published, without a title, as poem number 23 Williams's book *Spring and All* (Contact Publishing Co., 1923).

In the poem "That Which Makes Us Joyful", the four-line epigraph is borrowed from "Promise of Blue Horses" by Joy Harjo, from the book *How We Became Human: New and Selected Poems 1975–2001* (W. W. Norton & Company; Revised edition 2004).

The poem "Gently Let This Day" is inspired by the poem "Let This Day," from the book *Pax* by Annie Lighthart (Fernwood Press, 2021).

The poem "The heart is not" was written in response to a prompt in a James Crews Weekly Poem email. The prompt referenced the poem "The Heart Is Not," by Danusha Laméris, which appeared in *A Path to Kindness: Poems of Connection and Joy* (Storey Publishing, 2022), edited by James Crews.

About the Author

Marjorie Moorhead writes from a river valley, surrounded by mountains and four season change, at the border of NH/VT. She found a voice in poetry after surviving AIDS in its early years and becoming a mother. Much of her work addresses survival, environment, relationship, and appreciation of the everyday. She is the author of the chapbooks *Survival: Trees, Tides, Song* (Finishing Line Press, 2019) and *Survival Part 2: Trees, Birds, Ocean, Bees* (Duck Lake Books, 2020). Her poems have appeared in journals including *Amethyst Review, Tiny Seed Literary, Moist Poetry Journal, Bloodroot Literary, Sheila-Na-Gig, Porter House Review, Poeming Pigeon, Verse-Virtual, What Rough Beast,* and *The Poet's Touchstone*. Her poems are included in a number of anthologies, including those that benefit environmental, women's, Covid first-responder, and refugee aid organizations.

www.ingramcontent.com/pod-product-compliance
Lightning Source LLC
Chambersburg PA
CBHW022015160426
43197CB00007B/450